Steam Oven Baking

25+ sweet and stunning recipes made simple using your combi steam oven

EMILY RHODES

baking is a pleasure,
and the results bring joy
to those we share it with

Steam Oven
Baking

25+ sweet and stunning recipes
made simple using your combi steam oven

First Print Edition

also available in eBook format

Published by MacAllan Press, Australia

©Emily Rhodes 2021

Text, photography, design and formatting by Emily Rhodes

Print ISBN: 978-0-6452134-0-9
Ebook ISBN: 978-0-6452134-1-6

Visit Emily's website at steamandbake.com

Contents

INTRODUCTION

Baking probably isn't the first thing that springs to mind if you're new to the idea of combi steam oven cooking. Why, then, a steam oven baking book?

The hesitation many of you feel about this topic is exactly why I am so excited to show how helpful steam and combi steam can be to your baked goods. That, and the fact that baking is in my blood and I can just never get enough of pottering around in the kitchen with some butter, eggs and flour!

Dishes like custards and English style steamed puddings are obvious candidates for your steam oven, but so many other baked goods also benefit from the addition of steam. Breads, cakes and muffins come out tender and beautifully textured. Puff pastry becomes more flaky, with distinctive layers and great height. Even the preparation of frostings, fillings and sauces can be simplified or improved.

Within this collection of recipes, I hope you'll find not only some new favourites, but also more confidence and ideas to adapt your old favourites to this way of cooking.

Happy steam oven cooking,

AN IMPORTANT NOTE ON HUMIDITY (STEAM) LEVELS WHEN USING COMBI STEAM

The recipe settings in this book list a humidity level as well as an oven function (steam or combi steam) and temperature.

Many steam ovens have the option of selecting a humidity (or steam) level when using a combination steam setting. Some use percentages, while others have a low, medium, or high steam distinction. Some combi steam ovens have no option to alter humidity, offering instead a combi steam or convection steam function where the appliance determines the amount of steam dependent on temperature.

It is impossible to write recipes which cover the variable oven settings across all brands, so here's how to approach things if your oven doesn't use humidity percentages:

If you have a combi steam appliance with no option to select humidity or steam levels, simply use the combi steam setting and the oven temperature listed.
One of my own home ovens works this way, and all the recipes here have been tested in it multiple times with success.

If, instead of percentages, your appliance gives the option to select low, medium or high steam levels when you cook with combi steam settings, use the following guide to select the right option:

- Recipes calling for up to 40% humidity: low steam
- Recipes calling for up to 40-60% humidity: medium steam
- Recipes calling for more than 60% humidity: high steam

A NOTE ON COOKING TIMES

Because of the many ways combi steam ovens are manufactured, and their differing methods of providing steam for cooking functions, cooking times are always a guide. I am confident in all the recipes which follow but you do need to be mindful that in some ovens they may take a few minutes less to cook, others a few minutes more. Once you've been using your oven for a while, you'll find you can predict if dishes may cook faster or slower.

KITCHEN ESSENTIALS

Apart from my combi steam oven, I would not be without the following items in my kitchen when it comes to baking.

Stand mixer

I use a KitchenAid; the first birthday gift my husband ever bought me. It's still going strong many years later and was worth his investment (I hope he'd say the same given all the food I've made him with it!). I use it to mix doughs and batters, to whip cream and for lots of other tiresome mixing jobs.

A strong pair of hands and a spoon or whisk replace most of a mixer's tasks, but if you like baking a good mixer will never be overkill.

Food processor

Some sort of food processor or blender is handy for pureeing, but I frequently use mine to make pastry and chop or grind fruits and nuts, too.

Mixing bowls

The bowl I use most frequently is the one from my mixer. I also have an assortment of lightweight stainless steel bowls, a couple of glass ones and a Pyrex measuring jug. Anything which is large enough to contain your ingredients is just fine, although my preference is to stay away from plastic as it can hold smells from strong savoury or spicy foods and unleash them into your carefully prepared baked goods.

Measuring cups and spoons

One decent set of measuring cups with 1/4, 1/3, 1/2 and 1 cup is really all you need, and the same when it comes to spoons; a set with 1/4, 1/2 and 1 teaspoon plus 1 tablespoon sizes. Make sure you know whether your cup and spoon measures are US Customary/Imperial or Metric, as they differ slightly. It doesn't matter for many dishes but when it comes to baking, the difference between an American tablespoon (3 teaspoons) or a Metric tablespoon (4 teaspoons) can make a big difference to your results. I discuss measurements more on the Conversions page.

KITCHEN ESSENTIALS
CONTINUED

Spatulas, stirrers and whisks

Over the years I have pared down my collection of spatulas to a couple of favourites. I have two sizes of heatproof flexible silicone spatulas; these are shaped like shallow spoons with defined edges and are brilliant for mixing thick batters and scraping out bowls. The other stirring utensil I use frequently is an olive wood angled spatula, great for getting into the corners of saucepans.

Sometimes a whisk will be called for; I use a medium sized metal balloon whisk, bought from a catering store. Anything which has a handle that's comfortable to hold will work.

Baking trays and pans

Any ovenproof tray or pan can be used in your steam oven. For cake and muffin baking I keep a couple of 9x13in (23x33cm) rectangles, a couple of sizes of round cake pans and a muffin pan handy. For breads, one or two loaf pans are useful.

If you are baking pastry or dough in your combi steam oven, try to use dark coloured baking sheets and pans. They offer better browning to the undersides of your baked goods than light coloured metals. I have several dark metal cookie sheets and a few patty pan trays for little tarts and pies.

Most combi steam ovens come with a few stainless steel or enamel baking trays. These have the advantage of fitting perfectly into your oven but are rarely the size you need for baking.

Cast iron bakeware

I have a number of enameled cast iron pots; the most versatile is a low-sided Le Creuset pan with a domed lid. I use it almost daily for sweet and savoury cooking. It presents nicely going straight from oven to table, and the heavy material conducts heat incredibly well. I much prefer it to glass bakeware in most cases.

Microplane grater

I bought my first Microplane grater almost 20 years ago, and it's still going. I've now got 3 in total, of varying coarseness, though a single fine one would be sufficient! For ginger, spice grating and citrus zest they can't be beaten.

CONVERSIONS

Because I have a global readership, I allow for the two major units of measurement in all my recipes.

The recipes in this book are written using US Customary/Imperial measurements first and Metric measurements second.

I give oven temperatures in both Fahrenheit and Celsius in each recipe.

Please note that my recipes use metric cup and spoon equivalents.

There are differences in tablespoon and cup measurements between US Customary and Metric standards:

- 1 Metric tablespoon is 20ml, while US Customary/Imperial is 15ml.
- 1 Metric cup is 250ml, US Customary/Imperial is 240ml.

Readers using US Customary measures may take this into account by using 4 teaspoons where a tablespoon is called for, and slightly over-filling full cup measures.

GLOSSARY OF INGREDIENTS

Butter

I always use unsalted butter for baking and add salt separately. This gives more control over how salty (or not) a finished dish is.

If I call for 'soft' butter I mean something you can easily cut into cubes, but where the cubes will stay distinct and sharp-edged unless you squash them.

Occasionally a recipe might require 'very soft' butter, which is exactly what it sounds like. You should be able to squash very soft butter easily with the back of a spoon.

Superfine (caster) sugar

Identical in composition to granulated white sugar, but with much finer grains. I use superfine sugar in almost all my baking, it's far quicker to mix and dissolve than granulated sugar.

GLOSSARY OF INGREDIENTS
CONTINUED

Eggs

I use what are called extra large eggs in Australia. They average 60g (just a touch over 2oz). I always use free range or pasture-grown eggs for bird welfare reasons.

Flour

Unless otherwise stated, the recipes in this book refer to regular wheat flour. In the USA this is all-purpose flour, in Australia and the UK it's called plain flour.
For heavier doughs like breads, I sometimes call for bread flour. You can substitute all-purpose in a pinch, but bread flour (sometimes called baker's flour) has a higher protein content and develops a better gluten structure than all-purpose.

Vanilla Extract and Beans

I use vanilla a lot in baking. I always go for pure vanilla extract rather than synthetic vanilla essence. It's far more expensive but worth the splurge. The taste and aroma of real vanilla cannot be recreated by any synthetic product.
In some recipes I call for a vanilla bean with the seeds scraped out. Look for beans which are plump and soft; if they're dry and snap when you bend them, they're old and better used to scent a bag of sugar than for cooking.

Puff Pastry

I almost never make my own puff pastry. It's tricky and takes a long time. In Australia, pre-made and pre-rolled puff pastry comes packaged in square sheets measuring 30cm/12 inches. If you can't buy pre-rolled, look for a block of puff pastry at the supermarket or ask your local bakery.

Salt

Unless otherwise stated, I use fine-grained salt for baking.

Morning Bakes

Do breakfast or brunch in style, with baked goods
your loved ones will be dreaming about
all day

Apricot, Date and Seed Bread

Makes
1 x 8.5x4.5in (21x11cm) loaf

Oven Settings
To proof:
Steam/95°F/35°C/100% humidity
To bake:
Combi Steam/400°F/200°C/30% humidity

Prep Time
20 minutes plus proofing time

Cooking Time
30 minutes

I love a good fruit loaf for breakfast. Here, we're using apricots for tang and dates for sweetness. Equivalent weights of dried figs or raisins are also excellent. This is a great bread if you're new to yeast doughs, because proofing in your steam oven takes the guesswork out of how long to leave your dough to rise. I've also used instant yeast as it needs no pre-activating.

Ingredients
- 1 3/4 cups (225g) whole wheat flour
- 2 1/2 cups (350g) bread flour
- 2 1/2 tsp (1x7g sachet) instant dried yeast
- 1/4 cup (50g) granulated sugar
- ½ tsp salt
- 1 1/2 tsp ground cinnamon
- 1/2 tsp ground nutmeg
- 1/4 tsp ground cloves
- 1 tsp ground ginger
- 1 1/2 cups (375ml) water, lukewarm (you may need more)
- 2/3 cup (120g) dried apricots, roughly chopped
- 2/3 cup (120g) dried dates, roughly chopped
- 1/3 cup (45g) sunflower seeds
- 1/3 cup (45g) pumpkin seeds (pepitas)

Method
1. Put all the dry ingredients into the bowl of a stand mixer fitted with a dough hook. On low speed, mix in most of the water, keeping back a couple of tablespoons. Mix to form a soft, slightly sticky dough, adding a little more water if it seems dry.
2. Once the dough forms a mass, add the fruit and seeds and mix until everything is incorporated and the dough is smooth and elastic, around 6-8 minutes.
3. Turn the dough onto a lightly floured surface. Shape into a smooth ball and put it in a clean bowl. Put it in your steam oven at 100°F/38°C (use the dough proving setting if you have one) for 30 minutes. It should roughly double in size.
4. After the first rise, scrape the dough onto a lightly floured surface and press gently into a large rectangle. Fold it into thirds along the length of the dough, then roll tightly from one of the open ends to form a loaf. Put the loaf into your pan, tucking the ends downwards to keep a nice shape. Wrap the whole thing loosely in a plastic bag and put it in the fridge overnight – anywhere from 12-14 hours.
5. When you're ready to bake, take the dough out of the fridge while you preheat your oven. Preheat to 400°F/200°C/combination steam/30%.
6. Bake the bread for 10 minutes, then reduce the heat to 350°F/180°C (same humidity) for a further 20 minutes. The loaf should be golden brown all over and sound hollow when tapped.
7. Remove from the oven, turn out of the tin and leave to cool. The bread will keep, covered at room temp for a day or two, but is best sliced and frozen after that, ready for toasting.

Apricot, Date and Seed Bread

Sour Cherry and Cardamom Muffins

Makes
12 standard sized muffins

Oven Settings
Combi Steam/350°F/180°C/
30% humidity

Prep Time
5 minutes

Cooking Time
18 minutes

These muffins are fast to mix up and just a little unusual with earthy and fragrant cardamom and sour cherries. They're a great breakfast to go or lunchbox snack. If you can't get the sour cherries, dried cranberries make a great substitute.

Ingredients

- 2 cups (280g) all-purpose flour
- 3/4 cup (150g) granulated sugar
- 2 tsp baking powder
- 1 tsp ground cardamom
- 1/4 tsp fine salt
- 2 eggs
- 1/3 cup (85ml) vegetable oil or light olive oil
- 1/2 cup (125ml) whole milk
- 1/4 cup (60ml) plain yoghurt
- 1/2 cup dried (65g) sour cherries

Method

1. Preheat your oven to Combi Steam/350°F/180°C/30% humidity. Line a 12-hole standard sized muffin pan with paper cases, or grease well.
2. Put the flour, sugar, baking powder, cardamom and salt into a large bowl and give it a quick whisk to combine.
3. Put the eggs, oil, milk and yoghurt into a measuring jug or small bowl and whisk to combine well.
4. Pour the wet mix over the dry mix and stir until almost combined, with some streaks of flour remaining. Add the sour cherries and stir until just combined. The mixture does not need to be completely smooth; be careful not to overmix or your muffins will be tough.
5. Divide the mixture between the muffin holes and put the pan into the oven. Bake until the muffins are risen and golden brown, and spring back when pressed gently in the centre, about 18 minutes.
6. Remove the muffins from the oven and cool in the pan for 5 minutes. Turn onto a cooling rack. Eat warm or at room temperature. These muffins are best eaten on the day of baking, but can be warmed or toasted and spread with butter on the second day. Leftovers freeze well.

Variations
This muffin recipe is a great base for all sorts of different flavour combinations. To change things up, omit the cardamom and sour cherries and add between 1/2-3/4 cup of your favourite fruit (fresh, frozen or dried), chocolate chips or chopped nuts.

Sour Cherry and Cardamom Muffins

Dutch Baby Pancake

Makes
1 x 12in/30cm pancake, to serve 4

Oven Settings
Combi Steam/430°F/220°C/50% humidity

Prep Time
5 minutes

Cooking Time
30 minutes

Ingredients
- 4 large eggs
- 3/4 cup (90g) all-purpose (plain) flour
- 3/4 cup (185ml) whole milk
- 1/4 tsp salt
- 3 Tbsp butter

Baking this pancake is like performing a magic trick in your steam oven! Already impressive in a regular oven, Dutch babies literally go to new heights with the addition of steam, puffing into the most glorious airy pancake. I love to make these for weekend breakfasts because they're indulgent yet not too heavy (depending on your topping choices) and they require less time in the kitchen than a batch of regular pancakes.

This recipe calls for a round 12in/30cm heatproof pan; something with a heavy base is ideal. A 9x13in/23x33cm rectangular pan will work with the same amount of batter, although the shape means you may not get the same billowing heights as with a round pan.

Method
1. Put a 12in/30cm round pan into your cold oven and set oven to 430°F/220°C/ combination steam/40% humidity.
2. While the oven and pan are heating, put all the ingredients except the butter into a food processor and process until smooth. Alternatively, you can whisk the eggs by hand, then add the flour, milk and salt and whisk again until smooth.
3. When the oven has reached temperature, drop the butter into the pan to melt. Leave it for a couple of minutes until the butter is bubbling and just starting to turn golden.
4. Remove the pan from the oven and, working as quickly as you can, pour the pancake batter into the pan. The butter will slip and slide around and some of it may end up on top of the pancake batter – this is fine. Get the pan back into the oven as quickly as you can.
5. Cook the pancake until it's very puffy, rumpled and golden all over, about 12-15 minutes. Remove from the oven and add your toppings. Serve immediately.

Variations
The pancake can be served sweet or savoury, depending on what you choose to top it with. I've used fresh strawberries, cream and maple syrup, but there are plenty of ways to dress it up. Try:
- Lemon juice and a sprinkle of sugar
- Greek yoghurt, seasonal fruit and honey
- Nutella and raspberries or strawberries
- Shredded ham, cheese and chopped chives
- A great melting cheese like fontina or raclette
- Sauteed mushrooms mixed with a little cream

Dutch Baby Pancake

Fluffy Cinnamon Rolls

Makes
12 rolls

Oven Settings
To proof:
Steam/95°F/35°C/100% humidity
To bake:
Combi Steam/350°F/180°C/40% humidity

Prep Time
1 hour 30 minutes + proofing time

Cooking Time
25 minutes

Soft, fluffy and sticky, these rolls seem complex but are very straightforward to make. If you want fresh cinnamon rolls for breakfast without the early wake-up, prep through to step 6, then hold in the fridge overnight instead of going to step 7. In the morning, preheat your oven and bake straight from the fridge.

Ingredients
Dough
- 4 cups (480g) all-purpose flour
- 6 Tbsp (90g) unsalted butter, very soft
- 2 eggs
- 1 cup (250ml) whole milk
- 1 Tbsp granulated sugar
- 2 tsp instant yeast
- 1 tsp fine salt

Filling
- 3/4 cup (185g) unsalted butter, very soft
- 3/4 cup (150g) brown sugar, loosely packed
- 2 Tbsp ground cinnamon
- 2 tsp ground ginger
- 1 tsp ground allspice

Frosting
- 2 oz (60g) cream cheese, at room temperature
- 1/4 cup (60g) unsalted butter, softened
- 1 cup (125g) confectioners sugar
- 1 tsp vanilla extract
- 2 Tbsp whole milk

Method

1. Put the flour, butter, eggs, milk, sugar, yeast and salt into the bowl of a mixer fitted with a dough hook. Mix on low speed to combine, then increase to medium and mix until smooth and glossy, about 6 minutes. The dough will be very soft.
2. Put the bowl into your oven and set to steam/95°F/35°C/100% humidity (or use a dough proofing setting if you have one). Proof until the dough has doubled in size, about 40 minutes.
3. When the dough has doubled, turn it onto a lightly floured surface. Press out gently into a rectangle around 3/4 inch (2cm) thick. Wrap tightly in plastic wrap and freeze for 45 minutes-1 hour to allow the dough to firm up.
4. When the dough is firm, unwrap and place it onto the floured surface again. Roll it into a rectangle about 12x16 inches (30x40cm), then quickly and evenly spread the soft butter over the dough using the back of a palette knife. You want it to go all the way to the edges.
5. Mix the brown sugar, cinnamon, ginger and allspice together in a small bowl. Sprinkle the mixture over the buttered dough.
6. Roll the dough up tightly from the long side, to make a 16 inch (40cm) long log. Slice into 12 rolls and arrange in either a 12 inch (30cm) round or 9x13 inch (23x33cm) rectangle baking dish.
7. Set oven to steam/95°F/35°C/100% humidity and put the pan into the oven until the rolls are puffy and almost fill out the baking dish, about 30 minutes.
8. Leaving the dish in the oven, change the settings to combi steam/350°F/180°C/40% humidity, and bake the rolls until they're deep golden brown and risen, about 25 minutes.
9. While the rolls bake, make the frosting. Put the cream cheese, butter, confectioners sugar, vanilla and milk into the bowl of a mixer fitted with a paddle attachment and mix on low speed until well combined. Set aside.
10. When the rolls are cooked, remove from the oven and allow to cool for 5 minutes. Spread frosting over the top; it will soften and melt somewhat. Serve the rolls warm or at room temperature.

Fluffy Cinnamon Rolls

Pumpkin Bread

Makes
1 9x5in (23x13cm) loaf pan,
about 10 slices

Oven Settings
Combi Steam/340°F/170°C/30% humidity

Prep Time
10 minutes

Cooking Time
1 hour 5 minutes

Ingredients
- 15 oz (1 can) (400g) pumpkin puree
- 1 stick (115g) unsalted butter, melted
- 3 eggs
- 1 1/4 cups (250g) granulated sugar
- 2 1/4 cups (300g) all-purpose flour
- 1 tsp baking powder
- 1/2 tsp baking soda
- 1/2 tsp fine salt
- 1 tsp ground cinnamon
- 1 tsp ground ginger
- 1/4 tsp ground cloves
- 1/4 tsp ground white pepper
- 1 Tbsp granulated sugar, extra, for topping
- 1 tsp ground cinnamon, extra, for topping

This is one of my favourite quick breads, for its plush, even texture and toasty flavours.

A can of pumpkin puree is the fastest way to bake the loaf but I most often use home made puree because the taste and colour is deeper. To make your own puree, roast cubes of pumpkin on combi steam/400°F/200°C/50% humidity until they're very tender. Allow to cool slightly, then puree using an immersion blender. Make more than you'll need, it keeps brilliantly in the freezer for another loaf.

Method
1. Preheat your oven to combi steam/340°F/170°C/30% humidity. Grease a 9x5in (23x13cm) deep loaf pan and line with parchment paper, using enough paper so the long sides of the pan have some overhang. Clip the overhanging paper to the top rim of the pan with alligator clips.
2. Sift the flour, baking soda and powder, salt and spices into a large bowl and whisk to combine.
3. Put the pumpkin, melted butter, eggs and sugar into a large Pyrex measuring jug and whisk to combine well.
4. Make a well in the dry ingredients and pour in the pumpkin mixture. Mix thoroughly to combine, stopping as soon as the batter comes together or the bread will be tough.
5. Pour the batter into the pan, smoothing the top flat. Mix the extra sugar and cinnamon in a small bowl and sprinkle it evenly over the loaf, then bake until it's a deep golden brown and a skewer tests clean, about 1 hour 5 minutes. If you aren't sure whether it's cooked you can use a thermometer to check the internal temperature; it should read 200-205°F/93-96°C in the centre.
6. Remove the baked loaf from the oven and cool in the pan for 15 minutes, then turn out and allow to cool fully before slicing. Leftovers are fabulous toasted and buttered the next day, and extra slices can be wrapped and frozen.

Pumpkin Bread

Chocolate Chunk Banana Bread

Makes
1 9x5in (23x13cm) loaf pan,
about 10 slices

Oven Settings
Combi Steam/350°F/180°C/30% humidity

Prep Time
10 minutes

Cooking Time
55 minutes

Ingredients
Wet mix
- 3 very ripe bananas (medium/large, to give around 1 1/2 cups mashed banana)
- 1/2 cup/1 stick (115g) butter, melted
- 3/4 cup (145g) brown sugar
- 1 large egg
- 1 tsp vanilla extract

Dry mix
- 1 tsp baking soda (bicarbonate soda)
- 1/4 tsp fine salt
- 1 1/2 cups (200g) all-purpose flour (plain flour)
- 1 cup/6oz (170g) bittersweet chocolate, roughly chopped into pea-sized pieces

This is the banana bread to make when you want a no-holds-barred, deeply satisfying cake-style loaf with generous chunks of dark chocolate. It keeps for several days at room temperature and freezes well.

The puddles of chocolate in this loaf can make it difficult to test for doneness. If you have a probe thermometer it's easy enough to check using temperature instead of relying on guesswork or a skewer, though. When it's done, the center of the loaf should read 208-210°F/98-99°C with the probe inserted.

Method
1. Preheat your oven to combi steam/350°F/180°C/30% humidity. Grease a 9x5in (23x13cm) deep loaf pan and line with parchment paper, using enough paper so the long sides of the pan have some overhang. Clip the overhanging paper to the top rim of the pan with alligator clips.
2. Use a potato masher or fork to mash the bananas in a large bowl. Add the rest of the wet mix ingredients and stir well to combine.
3. Put all the dry mix ingredients except the chocolate into the bowl, then stir with a large spoon until it's almost mixed. Add the chocolate and stir in to just combine.
4. Scrape the batter into your lined pan and bake until it's risen, golden and tests clean with a skewer, about 55 minutes (if you'd like to bake to temperature doneness, the inside of the loaf should read 208-210°F/98-99°C with a probe inserted into the centre). Allow to cool in the pan for 10 minutes before turning onto a rack to cool completely.
5. Serve the banana bread in thick slices. I love it unadorned on the first day or two. After that I warm it slightly and spread with butter to serve.

Chocolate Chunk
Banana Bread

Healthier Fruit Crumble

Serves
4, generously

Oven Settings
Combi Steam/350°F/180°C/50% humidity

Prep Time
20 minutes

Cooking Time
25 minutes

Ingredients

- About 1.5lb (700g) ripe seasonal fruit, peeled if necessary and diced into 3/4in/2cm chunks
- 2 Tbsp granulated sugar
- 4oz/1 stick (115g) unsalted butter, chilled and cubed
- 1 cup (150g) whole wheat (wholemeal) flour
- 1/2 cup (50g) rolled oats
- 1/4 cup (50g) firmly packed brown sugar
- 1/4 tsp salt
- 1 tsp ground ginger
- 1/2 tsp ground cinnamon
- 1/4 cup/1.75oz (50g) pecans, roughly chopped

This recipe is a simplified, less-sweet version of a regular crumble, which makes it perfect for breakfast when you have an abundance of seasonal fruit. Almost any fruit goes; try apples, pears and rhubarb in winter and stone fruit or berries in summer. Basically, if you can stew or poach it, it'll work in this dish. Just know that firmer fruits may need a little more cooking time to soften.

As written, this will give you a crumble that's barely sweet, especially if you use a tart fruit like plums or rhubarb. You may need to adjust to taste.

If you'd like to bake this in individual servings, divide the mixture between 4 to 6 ramekins, and drop the cooking time by about 5 minutes.

I like to serve this with a big spoonful of unsweetened Greek yoghurt, which adds a cool and creamy, but not too rich, element to offset the fruit and crispy topping.

Method

1. Preheat your oven to combi steam/350°F/180°C/30% humidity.
2. Mix the fruit and sugar together in a bowl, then put into a 1 quart/1 litre baking dish.
3. Make the crumble. Put butter into a bowl with the flour, oats, sugar, salt and spices. Using your fingertips, rub the butter into the dry ingredients until it resembles damp sand. Mix the nuts through, then pile the crumble over the fruit. Don't press down, you want it to be quite loose.
4. Bake the crumble until the topping is golden and the fruit is collapsed and syrupy, about 20-25 minutes. Serve hot or warm; leftovers will keep a few days in the fridge and reheat well.

Teatime

Sweet treats perfect for coffee mornings
and afternoon pick-me-ups

Baked Custard Tarts

Makes
12 tarts

Oven Settings
Combi Steam/450°F/230°C/50% humidity

Prep Time
20 minutes

Cooking Time
17 minutes

Ingredients

- 1 batch of No-Stir Custard (page 62), chilled
- 2 sheets store bought frozen butter puff pastry, thawed but cold
- 1 1/2 Tbsp superfine (caster) sugar
- 1 1/2 tsp ground cinnamon

These delicious little tarts are inspired by the Portuguese Pastéis de Nata. The originals are created using a handmade, crisp layered pastry and sweet custard, baked hot and fast to create the telltale scorch marks on top of the tarts. My version is vastly simplified, made with bought puff pastry and my No-Stir Custard for the filling. It includes a hint of cinnamon, which I don't think is traditional; feel free to leave it out if you prefer.

The steam oven does a great job of making the pastry light and flaky here, and the humidity keeps the custard lovely and creamy. My tarts may not be as traditional as the classic Pastéis de Nata, but they are much easier to make at home and you won't have to visit Portugal to get them!

Make the custard for these tarts the day before so it's well chilled before you start.

Method

1. Preheat your oven to combi steam/450°F/230°C/50% humidity. Lightly grease a standard sized 12-hole muffin pan and put it in the fridge while you prepare the pastry.
2. Mix the sugar and cinnamon together in a small bowl. Sprinkle about half of this mixture over one sheet of pastry. Put the other piece of pastry on top and gently squash them together with a rolling pin. Sprinkle the remaining cinnamon sugar over the top, then roll the pastry tightly into a log. Trim the ends, then cut the log into 12 even portions.
3. Taking one piece of pastry at a time, place on your countertop with a cut side up and use the heel of your hand to flatten into discs which will fit most of the way up the sides of your muffin pan. Don't worry about all your swirls being evenly squashed, the unevenness is part of the appeal.
4. Give your chilled custard a stir to loosen and make it pourable, then divide it evenly between the pastry cases. It should come up to about 3/8in/1cm from the top of the pastry.
5. Bake until the pastry is puffed and golden, and the custard is lightly browned on top, about 17 minutes. During cooking the custard will puff quite dramatically; it'll sink and settle after you remove the tarts from the oven.
6. Remove the tarts from the oven and carefully lift them out of the pan using a small palette knife. Transfer to a wire rack to cool for 15 minutes, then serve warm. Don't be tempted to cool them fully in the pan as they'll be well and truly glued in by then!
7. These tarts are best eaten warm on the day you make them, but can be gently reheated in a dry oven if you have a few left over the next day.

Baked Custard Tarts

Burnt Butter Brownies

Makes
1 x 9x13in/23x33cm pan (24 pieces)

Oven Settings
Combi Steam/350°F/180°C/20% humidity

Prep Time
25 minutes

Cooking Time
18 minutes

Ingredients
- 12 oz/3 sticks (350g) unsalted butter
- 6 oz (170g) dark chocolate (55-70% cocoa solids), roughly chopped
- 2 cups (400g) superfine sugar
- 1/4 cup firmly packed (55g) dark brown sugar
- 1 tsp fine salt
- 6 eggs
- 2 tsp vanilla extract
- 1 cup (130g) all-purpose flour
- 1 1/3 cups (125g) Dutch process cocoa

As if brownies weren't rich and indulgent enough already, I like to take them to the extreme with toasty burnt butter. The butter adds depth, as does a combination of both cocoa and dark chocolate. Baking these in your steam oven increases the almost impossibly dense and chewy texture, and they cook a little quicker than in a regular oven. All the better to get them into your mouth faster.

Method
1. Lightly grease a 9x13in/23x33cm pan and line the base and long sides with parchment paper, using enough paper so there is some overhang from the top edges. Clip the overhanging paper to the rim of the pan with metal alligator clips.
2. Put the butter into a large, heavy based saucepan and cook on medium heat until melted. Increase heat to medium high and simmer, stirring frequently and scraping the bottom until the large, noisy bubbles have disappeared and been replaced by smaller, foamy bubbles. The milk solids should be golden brown. Remove from heat and immediately drop in the chocolate. Stir until it melts and set aside to cool slightly.
3. Preheat oven to combi steam/350°F/180°C/20% humidity.
4. Put the sugars, salt, eggs and vanilla into the bowl of a stand mixer fitted with the whisk attachment. Mix on medium high speed until very thick and fluffy, about 7 minutes.
5. While the eggs are mixing, sift the flour and cocoa into a medium bowl.
6. When the egg mixture is ready, reduce the mixer speed to low and carefully pour in the butter and chocolate. Leave the mixer running to fully incorporate, then switch off and add the flour and cocoa to the bowl. Mix on low speed until combined.
7. Remove the bowl from the mixer and give it one last stir by hand, getting to the bottom of the bowl to make sure it's evenly mixed right through.
8. Pour the mixture into the lined pan and bake until barely firm, about 18 minutes (if you'd like to bake to temperature doneness, the brownies should read 203°F/95°C with a probe thermometer inserted into the centre).
9. Cool the brownies fully in the pan, then carefully lift out using the overhanging paper and cut into squares. If you want very clean slices, rinse your knife between cuts.
10. Brownies will keep in a sealed container at room temperature for about 4 days. They can be frozen, well wrapped, for up to 3 months.

Burnt Butter Brownies

Vanilla Birthday Cake

Makes
1 x 9x13in/23x33cm pan (12-15 pieces)

Oven Settings
Combi Steam/350°F/180°C/20% humidity

Prep Time
15 minutes

Cooking Time
25 minutes

Ingredients
- 2 cups (290g) all-purpose flour
- 1 1/2 tsp baking powder
- 9 oz (250g) unsalted butter, softened and cubed
- 1 cup (200g) superfine sugar
- 3 eggs
- 1 tsp vanilla extract
- 3/4 cup (185ml) whipping cream

Sometimes the simplest sounding recipes are the hardest to get right; that was certainly the case with this classic vanilla cake! I wanted to create a cake that was pillowy, tender and even crumbed, and I failed numerous times with dense, heavy cakes or unevenly risen ones before I finally hit the jackpot with this recipe.

I'm glad I persisted because not only does it taste fabulous, this cake makes a perfect canvas for all kinds of frostings and decorations. And it cuts nicely, so it's ideal if you need a good sturdy 'base cake' to make a shaped novelty cake.

I frosted the pictured cake with my Cream Cheese Swiss Buttercream (p 66).

Method
1. Preheat oven to combi steam/350°F/180°C/20% humidity. Lightly grease a 9x13in/23x33cm pan and line the base and long sides with parchment paper, using enough paper so there is some overhang from the top edges. Clip the overhanging paper to the rim of the pan with metal alligator clips.
2. Put the flour and baking powder into a medium bowl and whisk to combine. Set aside.
3. Put the butter and sugar into the bowl of a stand mixer fitter with the paddle attachment. Mix on low speed to combine, then increase the speed to medium and beat until light and fluffy, about 3-4 minutes. Add the eggs, one at a time, fully incorporating each one before adding the next. Mix in the vanilla extract.
4. Take the bowl out of the mixer and use a spatula to gently mix in about a third of the flour. Mix in half the cream, then repeat to incorporate all the flour and cream. The mixture will be thick.
5. Scrape the batter into the pan and smooth the top. Bake until the cake is golden, risen and springy, about 25 minutes.
6. Remove the cake from the oven and cool for 5-10 minutes in the pan. Turn out and allow to cool fully before frosting.
7. This cake will keep, covered, for a couple of days at room temperature. After that, wrap well and freeze for up to 2 months.

Variations
- Lemon Cake: omit vanilla and mix in zest and juice of a large lemon with the butter and sugar.
- Raspberry Streusel Cake: rub together 2 oz (60g) cold unsalted butter with 1/4 tsp fine salt and 1/2 cup each brown sugar, granulated sugar and all-purpose flour, until it resembles sand. Scatter the cake batter with 3/4 cup whole raspberries and this mixture just before it goes into the oven.

Vanilla Birthday Cake

Lemon Ricotta Cake

Makes
1 8in/20cm round cake or
1 8½x4½in/20x12cm loaf

Oven Settings
Combi Steam /350°F/180°C/60% humidity

Prep Time
15 minutes

Cooking Time
40 minutes

Ingredients
- 3/4 cup (185g) unsalted butter, softened
- 1/4 tsp salt
- 1 1/4 cups (250g) superfine sugar
- 3 eggs
- 2 lemons, zested and juiced
- 1 lb (450g) ricotta cheese, firm, broken into 3-4 large chunks
- 1 1/2 cups (210g) all-purpose flour
- 1 1/2 tsp baking powder

This cake is close to my heart; it was the first recipe I ever posted on my website! Years later it's still a firm favourite and I'm happy it's stood the test of time. It's an unusual cake, with a dense texture somewhere between that of a regular crumb cake and a cheesecake. The ricotta lends creaminess without making it too rich and the lemon, possibly my favourite inclusion in any dessert, is bright and fresh.

Try to use a firm/drained ricotta in this recipe. Use something too wet and the cake will never seem like it's fully cooked, plus the large curds of a firmer cheese add a lovely texture to the finished cake. If you can't buy ricotta already drained, set it in a strainer over a bowl in the fridge overnight before making the cake.

Method
1. Preheat your oven to Combi Steam/350°F/180°C/60% humidity. Grease an 8in/20cm round pan or a 8½x4½in/20x12cm loaf pan and line the base with parchment paper.
2. Whisk the flour and baking powder together in a bowl and set aside.
3. Put the butter, salt and sugar into the bowl of a stand mixer and mix on medium speed until light and fluffy, about 5 minutes. Add the eggs one by one, mixing well after each addition.
4. Mix in the lemon zest and juice on low speed, then add the ricotta and mix briefly (don't mix it so the ricotta is completely smooth). The mixture will probably curdle when you put the lemon in. Don't worry, it'll come back together later.
5. Gently mix in the flour and baking powder until combined. It won't be completely smooth because of the ricotta but try not to leave any big clumps of flour.
6. Scrape the mixture into the lined pan and smooth the top. Bake until it's golden brown, puffed and tests clean with a skewer, about 40-45 minutes (if you'd like to bake to temperature doneness, the inside of the loaf should read 208-210°F/98-99°C on a probe thermometer).
7. Remove from oven and leave to cool in the pan for 30 minutes. Invert onto a wire rack to cool completely.
8. Serve barely warm or at room temperature with thick cream or yoghurt. The cake will keep for 4-5 days in the fridge and leftovers can be reheated after the first couple of days.

Carrot Cupcakes

Makes
12 cupcakes

Oven Settings
Combi Steam/350°F/180°C/30% humidity

Prep Time
15 minutes

Cooking Time
22 minutes

I have strong opinions about a good carrot cake recipe. The texture of the cake should be damp and dense but not doughy. There should be spices, especially ginger. Pecans trump walnuts. And, maybe contentious, but I think dried apricots are a far more worthy inclusion than raisins or sultanas. If you agree with all those statements, this is the carrot cake for you.

I frost this with my Cream Cheese Swiss Buttercream (p 66). It nods to the traditional carrot cake topping of cream cheese frosting but is a little less rich.

Ingredients

- 2 1/4 cups (300g) all-purpose flour
- 2 1/2 tsp baking powder
- 1 tsp ground cinnamon
- 1 tsp ground ginger
- 1/2 tsp ground allspice
- 4 eggs
- 1 cup (200g) superfine sugar
- 3/4 cup, lightly packed (150g) brown sugar
- 1/2 tsp fine salt
- 1 1/4 cups (300ml) vegetable oil (sunflower, almond or rice bran are my preferences)
- 4 oz (120g) pecans, chopped
- 5 oz (150g) dried apricots, chopped
- 2 oz (60g) candied ginger, finely chopped (optional but fabulous)
- 3 large carrots (about 300g), coarsely grated

Method

1. Preheat oven to Combi Steam/350°F/180°C/30% humidity. Grease a standard 12-hole muffin pan very well, or line with paper cupcake liners.
2. Put the flour, baking powder and spices into a large bowl and stir to combine.
3. In another large bowl, mix the eggs, sugars, salt and oil very well. Pour this into the dry ingredients and mix to combine.
4. Stir in the pecans, apricots, candied ginger (if using) and carrots, mix to combine well.
5. Divide the mixture evenly into the muffin pan and bake until the cupcakes are risen and golden brown, and spring back when pressed with a fingertip.
6. Remove from oven and allow to cool in the pan for 5 minutes before turning onto a rack to cool completely. When cool, frost with the Cream Cheese Swiss Meringue from p 66.
7. These cupcakes will keep, covered at room temperature for 2 days. After that, wrap and freeze for up to 3 months.

Carrot Cupcakes

Simple Steam Oven Chocolate Cake

Makes
1 9in/23cm layer cake, to serve 12

Oven Settings
Combi Steam/320°F/160°C/50% humidity

Prep Time
10 minutes

Cooking Time
20 minutes

This steam oven chocolate cake uses two bowls and a whisk. No melting, no beating, and, if you're lazy like me, not even any sifting. The key is baking the cake in layers for a fast, even cook which results in a soft, springy and even texture.

I love to frost this cake with my Favourite Chocolate Frosting (p 68), but my kids prefer it with Cream Cheese Swiss Buttercream (p 66) and sprinkles. Either way, we usually add a thin layer of berry jam with the frosting in between the layers.

Ingredients

- 2 cups (260g) all-purpose flour
- 1 cup (200g) superfine sugar (caster sugar)
- 1/2 cup (100g) dark brown sugar, firmly packed
- 3/4 cup (70g) Dutch process cocoa
- 2 tsp baking soda (bicarbonate soda)
- 1/2 tsp fine salt
- 1 cup (250ml) whole milk
- 1 tsp lemon juice
- 2 eggs
- 1 cup (250ml) vegetable oil (sunflower, almond or rice bran are my preferences)
- 1 tsp vanilla extract
- 1 cup water

Method

1. Preheat your oven to combi steam/320°F/160°C/50% humidity. Grease two 9 inch/22cm round cake pans and line the bases with parchment paper (use one pan, if that's all you have; you can turn out the first cake, pour the batter in for the second and bake in two batches. The second cake won't rise quite as much because the batter sits around longer, but the difference is negligible).
2. Put all the dry ingredients in a large bowl and give them a whisk to combine. I don't sift but if your baking soda or cocoa is lumpy, give it a quick sieve so you don't end up with poorly textured cake.
3. Put all the wet ingredients except the water into another bowl and whisk to combine. Pour the wet mixture into the dry mixture and whisk until just smooth. Add the water and stir to incorporate. The batter will be very thin.
4. Divide the batter between the two pans and bake until they're springy and test clean with a skewer, about 20 minutes. Leave to cool in pans for 5-10 minutes before turning out to cool completely. Fill, stack and frost when cool with one of the frostings from this book or your own favourite frosting.

Simple Steam Oven
Chocolate Cake

Tiny Pecan Pies

Makes
24 mini pies

Oven Settings
Combi Steam/350°F/180°C/50% humidity

Prep Time
15 minutes

Cooking Time
15 minutes

Ingredients

For the pastry
- 4 oz (115g) cream cheese, cold, cubed
- 4 oz/1 stick (115g) unsalted butter, cold, cut into 1/2in/1 1/2cm cubes
- 1 2/3 cups (225g) all-purpose flour
- 1/4 tsp salt

For the filling
- 1 cup (100g) pecans, roughly chopped
- 2 eggs
- 3/4 cup (150g) brown sugar firmly packed
- 1/2 tsp ground cinnamon
- 1/2 tsp ground ginger
- 1/4 tsp ground cloves
- 1/4 tsp salt
- 2 tsp bourbon (optional)

These itty bitty pecan pies are easy to make plus they keep and travel well, and I can just about guarantee they'll disappear off any dessert table faster than you can blink.

The easy food-processor crust for these pies is a little different than regular shortcrust pastry, using one of my favorite secret ingredients for tender pastry: cream cheese. No one will know it's there, but it makes a beautiful dough that's very easy to work with. I always make double the amount of pastry to use up a full block of cream cheese. If I don't need double the number of pies I just form the extra pastry into logs, wrap and freeze for up to a couple of months. Having the pastry on hand makes a batch of pies incredibly fast to put together on another day.

Method

1. Make the pastry. Pulse the cream cheese, butter, flour and salt in a food processor just until it forms a mass. Turn out onto a lightly floured surface and knead a couple of times to bring the dough together. Be careful not to overwork it.
2. Split the dough in half and form each half into a log about 2in/5cm in diameter. Wrap in cling film and refrigerate for at least 30 minutes.
3. While the pastry chills, make the filling. Put the eggs, sugar, spices, salt and bourbon into a jug and whisk with a fork to combine very well. Set aside.
4. When you're ready to bake, preheat oven to Combi Steam/350°F/180°C/50% humidity. Lightly grease two 12-hole rounded patty pan or muffin pans.
5. Slice each pastry log into 12 discs and use these to line the pans. If you're using muffin pans the pastry just needs to come ¾in/2cm up the sides, not all the way up. The pastry needs to make full contact with the pan bases so it browns properly; don't be afraid to manipulate and push it in really well. If there are any small holes or tears, just squash back together to make a smooth surface.
6. Divide the chopped pecans evenly between the pastry. Give the filling a quick stir to make sure it's mixed properly, then carefully pour it over the pecans so it comes almost to the top of each piece of pastry. Take your time; if the filling leaks over the edges it can be hard to remove the cooked pies from the trays later.
7. Bake until the pastry is golden and the filling puffed (it'll sink a little once you remove the pies from the oven, which is fine), 12-15 minutes. Cool the pies slightly, then turn out and serve warm or at room temperature.
8. The pies will keep for a couple of days, sealed, at room temperature. They freeze well for several weeks, just defrost at room temperature for a couple of hours. If you want to serve them warm, reheat using combi steam at 320°F/160°C/15% steam for 5 minutes.

Tiny Pecan Pies

Raspberry and Chocolate Loaf

Makes
1 9x5in (23x13cm) loaf pan, about 10 slices

Oven Settings
Combi Steam/350°F/180°C/25% humidity

Prep Time
10 minutes

Cooking Time
45 minutes

Like my favourite lemon ricotta cake on page 36, this one is dense and damp in texture. It's easier to make though, as there's no creaming involved. Just mix up all the wet ingredients in one bowl and the dry in another, then stir it together.

Ingredients

Wet mix
- 5 1/2 oz (150g) unsalted butter, melted
- 2 eggs
- 1 cup/7 oz (200g) plain yoghurt
- 1/3 cup (80ml) whole milk
- 1 1/2 tsp vanilla extract

Dry mix
- 3/4 cup (150g) superfine sugar
- 1 1/2 cups (200g) all-purpose flour
- 1 tsp baking powder
- 1/2 tsp fine salt
- 4 oz (120g) semisweet chocolate chopped into roughly pea-sized chunks
- 1/2 cup/3 1/2 oz (100g) frozen raspberries (don't bother thawing)

Method

1. Preheat oven to Combi Steam/350°F/180°C/25% humidity. Grease a 9x5in (23x13cm) deep loaf pan and line with parchment paper, using enough paper so the long sides of the pan have some overhang. Clip the overhanging paper to the top rim of the pan with alligator clips.
2. Put the melted butter, eggs, yoghurt, milk and vanilla into a medium bowl and mix well to combine.
3. Put the sugar, flour, baking powder and salt in another bowl and give it a quick whisk to combine. Pour in the wet mix and stir until it's almost smooth. Gently fold through the chocolate and raspberries, taking care not to overmix.
4. Pour the batter into the lined pan and smooth the top. Bake until the loaf is golden and a skewer tests clean in the centre about 45 minutes (if you'd like to bake to temperature doneness, the inside of the loaf should read 208-210°F/98-99°C with a probe inserted in the centre).
5. Cool in the pan for 10 minutes. Turn out onto a wire rack and cool completely before slicing.
6. The cake will keep, covered, for a couple of days, or can be frozen in individually wrapped slices for up to two months.

Variations
- Swap the raspberries and dark chocolate for blueberries and white chocolate and add the zest of a lemon.
- Use fresh strawberries instead of frozen raspberries.
- Swap the raspberries and dark chocolate for dried cranberries and milk chocolate chips.
- Swap the raspberries and dark chocolate for chopped dried apricots and white chocolate.

Raspberry and
Chocolate Loaf

Dessert

Indulge and impress
at casual weeknight
gatherings, special
occasions and
everything between

Lemon Delicious Pudding

Serves

4

Oven Settings

Combi Steam/350°F/180°C/40% humidity

Prep Time

15 minutes

Cooking Time

22 minutes

Ingredients

- 1/3 cup (80g) unsalted butter, softened
- 3 tsp finely grated lemon zest (from approx. 2 lemons)
- 1 cup (220g) caster sugar
- 3 eggs, separated
- 1/2 cup (70g) self-raising flour
- 1 2/3 cups (400ml) whole milk
- 1/3 cup (80ml) lemon juice (from approx. 3 lemons)

Almost like a cheat's souffle, this pudding bakes up into a fluffy, airy top layer with a thick, lemony sauce underneath. It's comforting and not too heavy, and as the name implies, absolutely delicious. Baking it in the steam oven is faster than using a regular oven.

I use self-raising flour in this recipe, which can be hard to find in the USA. If you can't get it, substitute the same amount of all-purpose flour and add 3/4 tsp baking powder.

Make sure you don't overbake this or it becomes more of a cake than a distinctly double-layered dessert.

Method

1. Preheat the oven to Combi Steam/350°F/180°C/40% humidity. Grease a 6 cup/1.5 litre baking dish.
2. Beat the butter, lemon zest and sugar with an electric mixer until pale. Beat in the egg yolks, one at a time, until thick, then stir in the flour, milk and lemon juice to combine. The mixture will look curdled, don't worry about this.
3. Beat the egg whites in another bowl using an electric mixer until they form stiff peaks. Gently fold through the lemon mixture, trying to keep the mixture light and stopping as soon as the streaks of egg white disappear. The batter may still appear a little curdled, but should be fairly homogenous. Pour the mixture into the prepared dish and bake until the top is golden and just barely firm to the touch (it should feel like a very underdone cake, not springy), about 22-25 minutes.
4. Serve immediately dusted with powdered sugar, with a jug of whipping cream alongside.

Lemon Delicious Pudding

Mascarpone and Raspberry Mille Feuille

Serves
8

Oven Settings
Combi Steam/350°F/180°C/60% humidity

Prep Time
30 minutes

Cooking Time
22 minutes

Ingredients
- 2 sheets (12in/30cm square) frozen all-butter puff pastry, thawed
- 1/2 cup (60g) confectioners sugar (icing sugar), plus a few Tbs, extra
- 8 oz (240g) fresh raspberries
- 1 cup (250g) whipping cream
- 1 tsp vanilla paste or a whole vanilla bean, split with seeds scraped out
- 7 oz (200g) mascarpone cheese

This flaky, creamy, lightly sweetened pastry tower is going to be something you come back to over and over. It's a great trick to have up your sleeve anytime you need to impress guests at short notice.

Method
1. Preheat oven to Combi Steam/350°F/180°C/60% humidity. Line 2 baking trays with parchment paper and set aside.
2. Cut each square of pastry into three strips, then cut each strip across into four rectangles, to give 12 pieces from each sheet (24 rectangles in total). Place the pastry on the lined trays, then cover each with another layer of parchment paper and a second tray to weight the pastry down. Cook for 9 minutes, swapping the trays around in the oven halfway through.
3. Remove the pastry from the oven and take off the top trays and paper layers. Dust the pastry with the extra confectioners sugar, then return to the oven until it's golden brown, about 10 minutes. Remove and cool. The pastry rectangles can be made to this stage up to 2 days before you need them; store between layers of parchment paper in an airtight container.
4. While the pastry cools, whip the cream with the vanilla paste and the ½ cup confectioners sugar until soft peaks form. Add the mascarpone and whip again just until the mixture is thick, then put the cream into a piping bag with a wide round nozzle. If you don't have a piping bag, a large plastic zip lock bag with one corner snipped off will do in a pinch.
5. To assemble, lay 8 of the pastry rectangles on a board and alternate dots of the mascarpone cream with the raspberries to cover. Place a second layer of pastry on top of each, then repeat the cream and raspberries before finishing with a final pastry layer. Dust the pastries with extra confectioners sugar and serve.

Mascarpone and Raspberry
Mille Feuille

Individual Dulce de Leche Cheesecakes

Makes
8 x 4oz/125ml cheesecakes

Oven Settings
Steam/185°F/85°C/100% humidity

Prep Time
15 minutes

Cooking Time
25 minutes

Perfectly portioned and so creamy, these cheesecakes are adaptable and a wonderful make ahead party dessert. You can freeze them, completely finished, and defrost overnight in the fridge before serving.

You'll need to cook the dulce de leche for these at least a day beforehand, so allow for that time.

Ingredients

- 4.5 oz (125g) digestive biscuits, graham crackers or other dry, sweet cookie, processed into crumbs
- 2 oz (55g) unsalted butter, melted
- 1 Tbsp granulated sugar
- 16 oz (450g) full fat cream cheese, room temperature
- 4 tbs superfine sugar
- 2 eggs
- 1 tsp vanilla extract or vanilla paste
- 3 Tbsp whipping cream
- 1 batch (14oz/400g) Dulce de Leche (recipe p70), or use bought dulce de leche

Method

1. Lightly grease 8 x 4oz/½ cup glass jars, or line 8 holes of a standard muffin pan with paper cases.
2. Set your oven to convection/350°F/180°C/0% humidity.
3. Mix the cookie crumbs and melted butter with the 1 Tbs sugar until it resembles damp sand. Divide the crumb mixture between the jars or muffin pan holes (it works out to about 1½ Tbs crumbs per cheesecake) and press down with the back of a spoon. Bake in the preheated oven for 10 minutes.
4. Remove the crusts from the oven, switch off and leave the door ajar to cool oven while you make the filling.
5. Put the cream cheese and sugar into the bowl of a food processor and blend just until smooth, then add the eggs, vanilla and cream and pulse until combined and smooth. Divide the mixture between the 8 prepared crusts and smooth the tops.
6. Set your oven to Steam/185°F/85°C/100% humidity.
7. Cook the cheesecakes for 25 minutes, or until set but with a slight wobble in the centre. Remove from oven, let cool to room temperature then refrigerate for at least 3 hours, or, covered, up to 3 days.
8. When you're ready to serve, warm the dulce de leche slightly to soften, then spoon a generous amount over each cheesecake and spread gently to cover. They need no other adornment but if you really feel like adding something, serve with a spoonful of whipped cream alongside.
9. Topped cheesecakes store well in the fridge for a day or two, or the freezer for a couple of months.

Variations
This recipe uses my steam oven Dulce de Leche from p 70, but you can change up the topping lots of ways. Try:
- Easy Citrus Curd on p 64
- Equal parts dark chocolate and cream, melted together to make a ganache
- Good quality berry or apricot jam
- Fresh fruit

Dulce de Leche
Cheesecakes

Crème Brûlee

Makes
6 x 4oz/1/2 cup (125ml) servings

Oven Settings
Steam/176°F/80°C/100% humidity

Prep Time
10 minutes

Cooking Time
1 hour

Ingredients

- 5 large egg yolks
- 1/2 cup (100g) granulated sugar
- 1/4 teaspoon fine salt
- 1 vanilla bean, split and seeds scraped
- 2 cups (500ml) heavy cream (35% butterfat)
- Approx 1/4 cup granulated sugar, extra, for tops

Traditionally cooked in a water bath, crème brulee has always been a little testy to get right. The ideal texture is softly set and creamy, but the unevenness of water bath cooking means it's easy to end up with brulee that's curdled or overcooked around the edges and unset in the middle.

Enter your steam oven, where you can select the exact temperature to set the eggs and achieve perfect edge-to-edge custard with very little effort. You can also steam these in jars with lids, if you like, which will pasteurise and seal the brulees so they keep up to 2 weeks in the fridge. The perfect make-ahead dessert!

If I'm serving these within a couple of days, I prefer to cook them in shallow ramekins because the ratio of crisp burnt sugar to custard is higher. I use small mason jars if I want to get ahead and cook them to keep.

Method
1. Put the egg yolks, sugar, salt, and vanilla seeds into a large bowl. Whisk together until well mixed, then slowly pour the heavy cream into the egg mixture, stirring to mix well.
2. Strain the mixture through a fine sieve, and slowly pour it into your ramekins or mason jars. Leave to sit for 15-20 minutes so any air bubbles come to the top and dissipate.
3. If you're using jars, place the lid on each jar and close gently until fingertip tight (this means the lid can be easily opened with 2 fingers).
4. Put the brulees on a baking pan and into your cold oven. Set to steam/176°F/80°C/100% humidity. Cook for 1 hour.
5. At the end of the cooking time, remove the brulees from the oven and allow to cool to warm before putting in the fridge to chill overnight. If you've used ramekins, cover the whole pan with foil once the brulees are cold.
6. When you're ready to serve, take the brulees out of the fridge and sprinkle about 1½ tsp extra sugar evenly over the top of each one. Using a kitchen blowtorch, melt and brown the sugar to a deep golden colour. If you don't have a blowtorch, broil/grill the sugar at the highest heat you can for a couple of minutes instead.
7. Let the caramelised sugar set for a minute or two, then serve immediately.

Variations
Switch up the flavour of your brulee with one of the following (omit the vanilla):
- 1 Tbs strong espresso coffee
- The zest and juice of a lemon or lime
- 1 Tbs amaretto liqueur

Creme Brulee

Steamed Jam Puddings

Makes
6 x 1/2 cup/125ml puddings

Oven Settings
Steam/212°F/100°C/100% humidity

Prep Time
15 minutes

Cooking Time
35 minutes

Ingredients

- 2/3 cup (200g) good quality jam
- 6.5oz (185g) unsalted butter, softened
- 3/4 cup (180g) superfine/caster sugar
- 3 large eggs
- 1 Tbsp milk
- 1 tsp vanilla extract
- 1 cup (150g) all purpose/plain flour
- 1 tsp baking powder
- Whipped cream or ice cream to serve

For a classic English style pudding, look no further. This dessert is comforting and traditional, with a lovely crumb and buttery flavour.

You'll need 6 half-cup molds for this recipe; I use metal pudding molds but heatproof teacups or even muffin pans would work. If you'd like to make a larger pudding instead, cook it in a 1 quart/1 litre pudding bowl and increase the steaming time to an hour and forty minutes.

Method

1. Grease the insides of 6 half-cup pudding molds. Divide the jam evenly between the bottoms of each mold and set aside.
2. Put the butter and sugar into the bowl of a stand mixer and mix on medium speed until fluffy. Add the eggs one by one, beating to incorporate each one before adding the next.
3. Mix in the milk and vanilla on low speed, then add the flour and baking powder and mix again until just combined. Give it one last mix by hand at this point, scraping to the bottom of the bowl to make sure there's no leftover flour.
4. Divide the mixture between the molds, then put them all into a baking pan and cover the top of the with foil (the foil doesn't need to be tight, it just prevents any drips from hitting the puddings as they steam).
5. Put the pan into your oven and set to Steam/212°F/100°C/100% humidity. Cook the puddings for 35 minutes, or until a skewer tests clean in the center of one.
6. Turn the puddings out and serve hot with whipped cream or ice cream.
7. These can be made and steamed ahead of time, they'll keep in the fridge for up to 2 days or in the freezer, wrapped individually in their molds, for up to 2 months. Thaw if frozen and reheat by steaming for 15-20 minutes.

Variations

- Swap the jam for treacle or golden syrup.
- Omit the jam layer and add a handful of golden raisins/sultanas to the pudding batter.
- Omit the jam layer and add the zest and juice of a lemon or an orange.

Steamed Jam Puddings

Classic Apple Tarte Tatin

Serves
6

Oven Settings
Combi Steam/430°F/230°C/60% humidity
then
Combi Steam/400°F/200°C/80% humidity

Prep Time
20 minutes

Cooking Time
45 minutes

Ingredients
- 2 sheets frozen all-butter puff pastry, thawed (12in/30cm squares)
- 2/3 cup (140g) superfine sugar (2/3 cup)
- 2 oz (60g) unsalted butter, cubed
- 1/2 tsp fine salt
- 5-6 whole cooking apples (Pink Ladies are my favourite)

One of the great French desserts, this showstopper tart is deceptively simple. The caramel-bathed apples and flaky pastry are made for steam oven cooking; the extra humidity makes the apples cook faster than usual and come out perfectly tender, and the pastry layers separate and puff higher than in a regular oven.

Be sure to cook the caramel until it just turns a rich amber color, you will have to watch carefully during this step as it turns quickly from golden to burnt and black.

Method
1. Put one sheet of pastry on top of the other and roll together. You aren't trying to make it a lot bigger, just create thicker pastry for more structure in your tart. Use a sharp knife to trim rounded corners. Imperfect trimming is fine, and you don't need to cut an exact circle as you're going to tuck in all the excess bits. Put pastry in the fridge until needed.
2. Preheat oven to combi steam/430°F/230°C/60% humidity.
3. Peel the apples and cut roughly into thirds. To do this, cut the pieces off close to the core and trim out any remaining seeds with a small knife.
4. Prepare caramel: sprinkle the sugar evenly over the base of a heavy 12in/30cm ovenproof skillet or casserole pan and bake until it's fully melted and turning a dark amber colour at the edges, about 15 minutes. The timing will vary depending on the heaviness of your pan and your sugar; watch closely as you want golden, not black.
5. Remove the pan from the oven and, working quickly to stop the sugar cooking, drop in butter and salt. It will sputter; let it die down then whisk to mix.
6. Change oven settings to combi steam/400°F/200°C/80% humidity.
7. Add the apples to the caramel and mix to coat. Don't worry if the caramel clumps and seizes, it'll soften again in the oven. Put the pan into the oven and cook for 8 minutes.
8. Remove the pan from the oven and use tongs to rearrange the apples cut side up in the pan so they are packed in tightly; this is easiest if you make an overlapping circle around the edge and then fill in the centre. It will seem like there are too many apples; that's what you want.
9. Working quickly, lay the pastry over the fruit and tuck the edges down all around. Cut a small vent in the centre of the pastry to release steam, then put the pan back in the oven and cook until the pastry is puffed and golden brown all over, about 25 minutes.
10. Remove the tart from the oven and let it sit undisturbed for around 30 minutes. Put a large plate upside down over the top of the pan and, using a kitchen towel to hold, invert the tart onto the plate. If any apples remain just lift out and place them back after you've turned it out.
11. Serve warm or at room temperature, with cream or ice cream. The tart is best eaten within a couple of hours of cooking.

Classic Apple Tarte Tatin

Basics

Custard, fillings and frostings
to take your bakes
to the next level

No-Stir Custard

Makes
Approximately 2 cups/500ml

Oven Settings
Steam/185°F/85°C/100% humidity

Prep Time
5 minutes

Cooking Time
1 hour

Ingredients

- 1 cup (250ml) pouring cream
- 2/3 cup (150ml) full fat milk
- 2 large eggs
- 1/3 cup (80g) sugar
- 1 vanilla pod, split and seeds scraped (optional)

This is a rich and silky custard, but if you'd like a custard that's even richer in flavor and color, switch one of the whole eggs for two yolks. To make it a little less heavy, replace some of the cream with milk.

If your jar is properly sealed, the custard will keep, unopened, for a couple of weeks in the fridge. Once opened it's best eaten within a few days. When serving, if you leave the custard cold and simply spoon it out of the jar it'll have quite a thick consistency, and if you stir well it'll become runny and pourable. For warm custard, just return the jar (or a portion of custard in a covered bowl) to the steam oven, using the same settings you cooked it on, and heat for 10-15 minutes before stirring and serving.

This recipe can easily be doubled or tripled. When I do so I use two or three jars rather than one larger one so cooking time can remain the same.

Method

1. Whisk together the cream, milk, eggs, sugar and vanilla (if using) very well. Strain through a fine sieve to remove any large bits of egg white, then pour into a 20oz/500ml or larger jar (or use two smaller jars). Put the lid on the jar and screw it closed to fingertip tightness (where the lid is closed properly, but not as tightly as possible). If you're using a canning jar with rubber ring and clamps, close with the ring and clamps in place.
2. Put the jar into your cold steam oven and set to steam/185°F/85°C/100% humidity. Cook for 1 hour.
3. At the end of cooking, remove from oven and cool to warm, then place into the fridge to chill. Properly sealed jars (where the rubber ring seal has vacuumed closed, or a screw top lid has inverted) will keep unopened in the fridge for a couple of weeks. Once opened, use the custard within a few days.

No-Stir Custard

Easy Citrus Curd

Makes
Approximately 1 1/2 cups

Oven Settings
Steam/175°F/80°C/100% humidity

Prep Time
10 minutes

Cooking Time
35 minutes

Ingredients

- 3.5 oz (100g) butter, melted
- 1/2 cup (100g) granulated sugar
- 1/3 cup (85ml) freshly squeezed lime juice (from about 3 limes)
- 1/3 cup (85ml) passionfruit pulp (from about 3 passionfruit)
- 2 eggs
- 2 egg yolks

I love citrus curds of all types, and this recipe is a great base to cover them all! Fresh and fragrant with lime and passionfruit, you can vary using any of the ideas below to create your own favourite. These quantities make a sharp curd but if you'd prefer yours to sit more on the sweet end of the scale, reduce the total fruit juice/pulp down to half a cup.

You can increase the quantities of this without much trouble at all. I've gone up to a quadruple batch and the only difference was that it took some extra time in the oven.

Use this on toast or to fill or top cakes, tarts and cookies. Cooked curd will keep, covered in the refrigerator, for about a week. I dare you not to eat it all before then.

Method

1. Put all the ingredients into a heatproof bowl. I like glass because I can see everything that's going on. I don't usually recommend glass for steaming because it conducts heat poorly, but it's going to be in there for a while so it'll get up to temperature fine. Whisk to combine well, but don't worry if the melted butter seems to settle on top when you stop whisking.
2. Put bowl into your steam oven and set to 175°F/80°C, steam setting (full steam/100% humidity). There's no need to cover the bowl. Steam the curd for 15 minutes, then stir well and return to the oven for a further 20 minutes or until thickened to your liking. The curd will noticeably thicken when the overall temperature reaches about 170°F/76°C, and continue to do so up to the oven's temperature of 175°F/80°C.
3. When the curd is done, pass it through a fine mesh strainer set over a bowl or jug, before storing in a well-covered container or lidded jar in the refrigerator.

Variations

- Lemon curd: replace the lime and passionfruit with the zest of 2 lemons and 2/3 cup lemon juice.
- Blood orange curd: replace the passionfruit with blood orange juice, leave the lime or substitute lemon so it doesn't become too sweet.
- Grapefruit curd: replace the lime juice with lemon juice and the passionfruit with pink grapefruit juice.

Easy Citrus Curd

Cream Cheese Swiss Buttercream

Makes
Approximately 5 cups

Oven Settings
Steam/150°F/65°C/100% humidity

Prep Time
25 minutes

Cooking Time
15 minutes

Ingredients
- 6 large egg whites (approximately 240g)
- 2 cups (400g) superfine sugar
- 12 oz/3 sticks (350g) unsalted butter, softened but cool, cut into Tbs sized pieces
- 2 tsp vanilla extract
- 1/8 teaspoon salt
- 4oz (115g) full fat cream cheese, room temperature, cut into Tbs sized pieces

Of all the recipes in this book, this is the one I really debated including. It's not as simple as most of the others, requiring some technique and careful handling, as well as a good stand mixer. The results are so worthwhile, though. With a little attention to detail, you'll end up with a soft, silky and rich buttercream that's not too sweet and pipes like a dream. The addition of cream cheese gives it a deeper and more interesting flavour, although feel free to stop just before adding it, in which case you'll have a lovely regular Swiss meringue buttercream.

The quantities here give a sizeable batch of buttercream, enough to easily fill and frost a two or three-layer cake. If you don't need it all, it keeps well in the fridge or freezer for another time. And all the leftover egg yolks from those whites? Use them to make custard (p 62) or citrus curd (p 64)!

Method
1. By hand, whisk the egg whites and sugar together in the bowl from a stand mixer (make sure the bowl is spotlessly clean). Put the bowl into your oven and set to steam/150°F/65°C/100% humidity. Cook for about 15 minutes, whisking a couple of times. The mixture will start out grainy from the sugar; what you're doing here is heating the egg whites and dissolving the sugar. It's done when you can rub the mixture between your thumb and finger and not feel any sugar granules.
2. Transfer mixture to a stand mixer fitted with a whisk attachment. Whip the mixture on medium high speed until stiff, glossy peaks form and the meringue is no longer warm to the touch, 10-15 minutes. If the meringue is done and the bowl is still warm, switch off your mixer and leave to cool to room temperature before you proceed to the next step.
3. Turn the mixer back on to medium high speed and add the butter, 1 piece at a time. Wait for each piece to fully mix in before adding the next. After all the butter has been added, turn the mixer down to medium speed and beat in the vanilla and salt. If you want a standard Swiss meringue buttercream, stop here, you're done! For the cream cheese version, proceed to the next step.
4. Leaving the mixer running, add the cream cheese one piece at a time, just as you did for the butter. Once it's mixed in and the buttercream is smooth, stop mixing.
5. Use the buttercream straight away or leave, covered, at room temperature, for up to 6 hours. If you want to store for later, put it into an airtight container and wrap very well, then refrigerate up to 4 days or freeze up to 2 months. To bring it back to life, let it come to room temperature again and beat for 2-3 minutes until creamy before using.

Cream Cheese Swiss Buttercream

My Favourite Chocolate Frosting

Makes
Approximately xx cups

Oven Settings
Steam/115°F/45°C/100% humidity

Prep Time
5 minutes

Cooking Time
25 minutes

Ingredients

- 1 lb (450g) bar or block dark chocolate (50-65% cocoa solids), chopped into pea-sized pieces

- 14 oz (400g) full fat sour cream, room temperature

My absolute favourite chocolate frosting is so easy to make and only contains two ingredients; maybe three if you want to add a touch of vanilla or salt. It's rich, glossy and deeply chocolatey with a pronounced tang which balances the sweetness of both frosting and cake. Use any dark chocolate you like, just make sure you're happy to eat it as the flavour does come through. My preference is Callebaut 54% Dark.

I use this to frost my Simple Steam Oven Chocolate Cake (p40), and occasionally the Vanilla Birthday Cake on p34. It's also great as a filling for sandwiching cookies together, and if you like frosting on your brownies it's sturdy enough to match the density of those. I wouldn't recommend using it on a light sponge-type cake as it's a little heavy.

This frosting spreads beautifully not long after you've made it and sets quite firm on cooling. If it's too thick to spread, just re-warm and stir well until it's the consistency you're after.

Method

1. Put the chocolate and sour cream into a heatproof bowl and cover tightly with plastic wrap. Put it into your oven and set to steam/115°F/45°C/100% humidity. Cook until the chocolate is completely melted. Stir gently a couple of times during this process, making sure to re-cover the bowl tightly after each stir so no moisture gets in. Depending on your bowl shape and size, this step will take 20-30 minutes.
2. When the chocolate is melted, remove the bowl from the oven and whisk well until completely smooth. The frosting will be quite thin at this point, and thickens as it cools. You can use it immediately if you want a thin, pourable frosting, or whisk every now and then as it cools until it's the consistency you want to use.
3. Store the frosting at room temperature with a layer of plastic wrap pressed onto the surface for up to 6 hours. After that, it keeps in the fridge for up to a week but will need to be rewarmed and whisked to bring it back to a usable consistency.

My Favourite Chocolate Frosting

Decadent Dulce de Leche

Makes
14oz/400g

Oven Settings
Steam/185°F/85°C/100% humidity

Prep Time
5 minutes

Cooking Time
12 hours

Ingredients

- 1 x 14oz (400g) can full fat sweetened condensed milk

If you're as much a fan of caramel as I am, this recipe is going to be dangerous. Dulce de Leche is popular throughout South America, and is made by very slowly cooking sweetened condensed milk until the sugars darken and everything thickens into a sticky, rich caramel.

Dulce de Leche can be cooked on the stovetop, where you have to stir and watch carefully to make sure it doesn't burn, or boiled in the can, which carries an explosion risk. No thanks. Here I take the hands off approach of slowly steaming, which results in perfect caramel every time.

I'm sure you'll figure out what to do with this, but if you need any ideas, I use it to fill layer cakes, spoon over ice cream and sandwich butter cookies. I have also been known to sneak it by the spoonful.

This recipe is easily doubled, you just need an extra jar or two. It keeps, unopened in the fridge, for several weeks.

Method

1. Preheat oven to steam/185°F/85°C/100% humidity. Have a 14oz or larger canning jar, or a couple of smaller jars, clean and ready to use.
2. Open the can and pour the contents into your clean jar/s. Put lids on and close to fingertip tight (this means the lid can be easily opened with 2 fingers).
3. Put the jars into the preheated oven and cook for 12 hours. I generally set my oven to go overnight for this recipe. If you want to do the same and your oven is not plumbed, make sure your water tank will last the night without needing a refill (most will go for several hours at this temperature, but will almost certainly need a refill at some point during cooking).
4. At the end of cooking, remove the jars from the oven. Cool to room temperature and then place in the fridge until you're ready to use. Once opened, use the contents within a few days.

Decadent Dulce de Leche

Visit
steamandbake.com
for hundreds more
steam oven recipes
and other cookbooks

Printed in Great Britain
by Amazon

28014079R00043